FAITHFUL

CLIFF ASHCROFT
FAITHFUL

CARCANET

First published in 1996 by
Carcanet Press Limited
402-406 Corn Exchange Buildings
Manchester M4 3BY

A CIP catalogue record for this book
is available from the British Library
ISBN 1 85754 258 4

The publisher acknowledges financial assistance
from the Arts Council of England

Set in 10 pt Sabon by Bryan Williamson, Frome
Printed and bound in England by SRP Ltd, Exeter

For Ruth

Acknowledgements

Some of these poems first appeared in the following magazines and anthologies: *Affinity, The Independent, New Poetries, PN Review, The Spectator, Stand, The Times Literary Supplement.*

I am grateful to Chatto & Windus for permission to quote from C.P. Cavafy's poem 'King Dimitrios' from his *Collected Poems* translated by Edmund Keeley & Philip Sherrard, edited by George Savidis.

In the prose-poem 'Faithful' I am indebted to Norman Cohn's *The Pursuit of the Millenium* (Temple Smith, 1970) for details of the siege of Münster.

Contents

I Utopians

Taborites

During the unrest which came to our country
the insurgents called themselves Taborites
after giving the biblical name Tabor to their town on the hill.

They took their families and belongings
to the bare escarpments and began an endeavour
that was to last my exceptional childhood.

At the time I knew nothing of the second coming,
though the community moved, as I remember,
with a purpose and excitement I have never found since.

Christ was expected in the dress of a brigand.
So the local thieves were received with joy,
and though lacking the holy credential

still gave up crime for the plenty and good living
we heaped upon them, just in case.
We tilled our land and built our dwellings

simply, but to last. For it was obvious now
we would live forever, and the children born to us
would slip from their mothers like ships out of harbour.

For some the millenium had already arrived,
wandering through the woods naked and dancing.
They were in a state of innocence.

But for me, it was only later,
when the authorities had sequestered our land,
that I remembered my brothers and sisters

singing in the green woodland.
Now the local farmers who have taken me on
comment sourly on the local simpleton

who strips off his clothes in the cornfields nearby.
They tap their skulls and shake their heads sadly,
for he is mad and beyond redemption,

who can restrain him now
the boy thinks he has entered heaven.

Digger

It was April, the buds pressed out of the branches
and I was afraid of the sallow villagers.
My friends eased me, saying 'the earth
is our common treasury, you share of anything we grow,
of any joy or misfortune we possess',
and their hands at night about the fire.

We had dug-up and manured the wasteland,
planting beans, wheat and rye, parsnips and carrots
before sinking onto our backs for the productive purpose
of our lives there, in study and recreation.
But one morning, as I expected,
we woke to find the field trampled and broken,
our outlying huts smoking, pulled to the ground,
my own tools pitched into the ruined walls.
As I watched the rain tick over my boots
I thought my time is spent starting over and over.
When will anything I begin complete its life?

Our crime was boldness and happiness.
And for that we could never be allowed to rest.
The timid, miserable villagers set their faces
and in darkness destroyed what maintained our difference.
Now under the local militia we share
the same reassuring meanness of spirit.

Sourness beats out the light in the eyes.
I do not dig the wasteland anymore.
Everything is hard won, and the price
of one acre of peaceful land
is a war to surround it.

King of the Last Days

The sun soaks into my room like a flood of amber.
It blankets him, sleeping softly by the closed door –
still hugging the velvet cloak we laid upon his shoulders.
His poor crown turns slightly in the litter about my feet.
I hope he will wake soon. I hope he will rise
of his own accord because today is the day
that everything we have waited for will happen.

I would get up to wash, to clean this grime from my face
and wait quietly for his voice to summon me.
But now there is no use in all that service, even waking
will not matter to us. The sun rises on its last
incomplete arc and I pin-point where in the sky
it will make its sharp and final descent.

I feel a farewell warmth prick the fingers of my resting hands.
The king snuffles into his ermine. I am a little sorry
for us, thinking of it now at this early, bright hour;
sorry that our anticipation must end
and my employment is over. There can be no more coronations,
no more holy marriages, our lives are finished or fulfilled
now the dark hand he promised must come to gather us.

Faithful

Because I was born out of wedlock and was taught no trade except how to use my fists for food, I joined the Bishop's mercenaries and began the slow march to encircle a walled and obscure town. I was told that the inhabitants believed that like the radiance of the sun, which fell on everybody, so their food and possessions, even their marriages were to be held in common – and also a passion burnt in them for the world's drastic and imminent end. The situation was familiar and I concerned myself with the completion of my military term, its pay and regular food.

We began the blockade in January. There was to be no fighting. No food entered the city for some weeks. Eventually we heard the sounds of horses gone to slaughter – also the terse declamations of their leader as his last great banquets ended in music then sudden silence. By April the town was in famine. Every dog and cat had been killed and eaten. They say they ate moss, old shoes, even the whitewash from the walls; but I saw nothing of this. What I had been stationed to witness was still waiting for me. Their leader said they would all be saved by Easter, if not, let him be consumed by flame. He also said he would change the cobblestones to bread. But when the communal graves were overflowing and his chosen people had not taken food for eight weeks, he agreed to free those who wished to leave his hands.

The Bishop's instructions were clear. Should any of the populace leave the town gate, slaughter the men first, refuse to allow the women and children to pass our blockhouses. My job was simply the familiar and rapid violence then the leisured brutality of watching these people crawl from our swords to the city's closed gate. They would cry up to me and eat grass like animals at my feet. Despite the promises they received of blessedness on death, they scraped the town gates for entry into a hell they preferred to our stiff faces and the strip of land like an open grave.

So they died, and when the Bishop ordered us to breach the high walls, all we found was silence and the pitiful bodies heaped like rags in the stripped quarters. Even their great leader we scraped like common dust into a sack, placing his jewellery, mitre and cloak to one side for the Bishop's disposal. I returned to barracks for my last meal, clothes and final discharge.

The Bishop was congratulated on the success of his campaign, and certainly our payment was above what I could normally expect at that location and in those times. I find the Church, to its credit, hires with little concern for my birth or station in life and is always a good and regular employer.

Anselmo's Revolutionary Pamphlets

The austere printer Anselmo Lorenzo
carried the message from village to village
and awakened me with a clear word.
A word that pressed upon my open hands
and fired a pure and supple flame.

I too dreamed of the *el reparto*,
the re-distributed land, our fields returned
like the warm acre of our village beds.
And the landowner and priest fell from
my memory like winter's evil cold.

Anselmo Lorenzo I think of you
leading us from the certainty of punishment
into the doubt of our free limbs.
What was to become of us now
we could do exactly as we wished?

I looked for your word in my frozen hands,
but there will be no simple rest.
All you have brought is empty dispute
and the cinders I press to my closed palms
like letters of broken type.

Midsummer Morning (1936)

They met in a pink-washed room at the back of the bar
and talked of the new world to come
where each man was his own private government,
and the palaces of this world not unlike here
with its litter, beer and meagre food.

They were such simple men. I was laughing when the destroyers
dropped their chains in the open bay.
All the villagers could do was shuffle onto the cinders
and watch each private government make its silent exit
under the darkness of their sallow faces.

I thought that was that, and returned to the bars
for cards and wine and the end of my travelling.
I wanted a sleeping province and confirmation of the sour taste
that assailed me in England, in France, in Spain.

They were all gathering on that cinder shore.
They all wanted the relief of that invincible force
massed like a deep and secure wall
around our oceans, our hillsides, our towns and greens,
even the windows of our own rooms.

Sometimes Anselmo would come, his coat stuffed with pamphlets.
He would carefully spread them over the card table
like a decisive hand that must win him the game.
And though they were crude, roughly printed affairs
which I quickly read and ignored,

the men pored over them, stroking the letters,
slowly spelling out the words that meant, in the end,
I would have to leave them.
Theirs was a simple but useless game.
Like a gracious liner travel called me,
proclaiming sweetness, sea and freedom,
while the villages I visited fell in grey chains behind me.

Barbers

In Spain the barbers were Anarchists.
Mr Blair thought it queer, in the barber's shop,
to see the notice on the wall
explaining that tips were prohibited:
'The Revolution has struck off our chains.'

In Blackpool, Mr Greasley had not heard of his Spanish brothers.
He was a polite dictator, knowing only one severe order
which, as children, we had to obey.
After sentence, he would pocket his unprohibited pennies
and pick up the fags he smoked in chains.
The good news had not reached him,
and the only red he ever displayed
span on his barber's pole.

Conscript

Now the room has been emptied of its contents
and the shelled house abandoned. I inherit
one small saucepan and a plastic bowl.
I open the cans pennies have bought me,
with nails prised from the kitchen sill.
All this week it has rained.

Everything here is washed-out purple –
the torn bedspread and sheet, the damp pillowcases,
even the wallpaper with its bold design
echoes the photographs of Yugoslav royalty
that litter the floor. Here is the king
on his wedding day, and here,
smiling and eager for his confirmation.

I remember some girls at the station
gave me bags of shrunken oranges.
All their fathers were dead, they said.
Yes, they were dead, sleeping alone,
cold because they had cursed God,
cursed the King, fled and were shivering now
in an abandoned place without food or warmth.
They, however, would not do such a thing.
They would volunteer and fight, like me.

My ration of grey bread did not help.
Escape lay ahead like a black corridor.
I followed it with eyes shut, taking the oranges,
smiling for the girls, raising my hand,
not to slaughter and hollow defeat, but to me.

The Byzantine Mary watches me curl
into my stiff clothes. She has a gold room,
and silver feet. And though the frame is shattered
she smiles a taut and painted smile.
She has volunteered, like the king
at confirmation and the daughters at the station,
all have volunteered, and unlike me
can never leave their abandoned home.

II Christians

Cana

I was at a wedding where
there was dancing and music, but no drink.
And because I knew nobody there
I missed the alcohol, turning to the seafront
and my boredom.

There was a great noise in the house,
a sort of shout, which to me in my abstraction
sounded like neither joy nor terror.
I did not turn around.
Everything that had stopped seemed to continue.

Someone came up to me and gave me a glass.
I was tired of water and juice,
tired of my sobriety.
But I took the glass because, if anything,
I am obedient and polite.

'Here is some wine,' she said.
And at the beat of my host's breathing,
the great wedding company called me in,
not to face the floor and the dust on my knees,
but to drink and to dance.

Bethesda

'Now there is at Jerusalem by the sheep market a pool,
which is called in the Hebrew tongue Bethesda, having five
porches. In these lay a great multitude of impotent folk, of
blind, halt, withered, waiting for the moving of the water.
For an angel went down at a certain season into the pool,
and troubled the water: whosoever then first after the
troubling of the water stepped in was made whole of
whatsoever disease he had.'

(John V, v.2-4)

The moving of the water.
I lay still on the ground.
Everybody else was facing the other way
calling out to travellers, give alms,
I am sick, give alms, give alms.

I had been ill for so long.
My voice was faint and
I could not move my legs or arms.

A woman came, middle-aged, bent,
labour and thrift marked her.
She set her basket down and began to undress.
I did not cry out, lady you can't do that here,
this is a holy place, leave me some bread and go.
I said nothing.

She stripped completely and her skin was loose,
but her back suddenly erect and shaped
as she stepped quietly into the water.
She eased forward and stretched out full into the pool
and began to swim across the length.
She disappeared into the dim at the rear,
and I lost her, my eyes accustomed so to the sun
and staring up at the walking people and their purses.
But she returned soon enough, rising out of the water
onto the green steps and back into her clothes.

Nothing seemed to have happened.
I knew swimming in the pool was a serious offence.
I was not going to say anything,
except for a query to God for a plain sight
of troubled water and no able arms or legs
to carry me there.

John XXI, v.9

As soon as they came to land
they saw a fire of coals there,
and fish laid upon the coals
and some bread.
But the preparer of the meal
was not to be seen.
So they ate their fill,
and the fish seemed to feed them gladly,
and there was still meat upon the bone,
and crusts multiplied from the single loaf.
And the men lay their damp, salt clothes
to one side and slept under the high sun,
heedless, content from the meal.

So the afternoon passed,
and I came upon the disciples naked and sleeping
like children worn out from the day's play,
at peace, and I had not the heart to wake them.
They lay as in a tangled faceless crowd
before turning their eyes to the palms of their hands
for that familiar place of rest.
So the still bodies were sleeping
by the dying coals, the crusts and bones.

Is it time now for us to rise
and turn to the city walls with their market places
and synagogues, their auditoriums and palaces;
or are we keepers of the small fire
inviting, as with a simple gesture of the palm,
the lake-side, the fish, the broken bread?

John IX, v.6

And the great crowd began to disperse,
still in high ferment, exclaiming, some shouting.
Even our local traders turned their eyes
to the city gates, not to their goods.
I took my courage then and pushed forward
to the quiet circle surrounded only by turned dust.

I'd always thought from my father's tales
that being present at some marvellous occasion
I would be in a high auditorium,
or among brilliant banners, with the din of horns
and loose drums about my ears,
a prince shining as he declaimed.
But there was only dust here and small pats of mud.

As a grown man my mother took me to the water-side
to point out how large and bright the collection of boats
had been that especial year, and how she had collected
the fallen belongings of each man who had left that crowd
changed, and the knife or coin no longer considered.

My memory has never turned on the great stadiums,
the avenues of stretching hands,
never considered the silver arcades
within each prince's promenade, only fixed
to a circle of dust, a pair of sudden blue eyes,
and the mud I did not pick up.

John IV, v.6

I cannot say if my information is correct,
the borders of my memory grow grey and unclear.

My friend, who is not from this place went to draw water.
A man, sat by the well, asked her for some.
She was surprised as her treatment by him was not the way
of people here; was civil, even courteous.
I sat in my chair to watch. I couldn't hear his responses,
but hers, so clear and typical, came singing out towards me.

'Sir, have you nothing to draw with, the well is deep,
from where did you get this living water?
If I take this water will I never grow thirsty,
will I never have to draw from this well again?
Give me some of this water, cool, clear,
resting at the bottom of all things, steady,
not like my hands that shake and wither.

'I am afraid of growing old.
I sit at night in my snug quarters,
a guest in the house crying because
I cannot eat the meat given to me,
such is my heart's presence high in my throat,
choking me, and at night my body is not still.

'Come morning I have had dreams I do not understand.
Will you understand them? If I tell them,
will you interpret for me? They are reckless, fraught,
I cannot hold my head up in the street.
You are a stranger and I trust you already.
Your smile is full of trust, I answer to that.
I won't let you forget me, I will tell people
about you in the city, though they think me mad.
I will wear white as a banner.'

The talk would not stop coming from her.
The man only continued to listen,
slowly drawing up the pail she had forgotten.

Our Father

'Tiberius Julius Abdus Pantera of Sidon,
aged 62, a soldier of forty years service,
of the 1st cohort of archers, lies here.'

He never actually saw the stone.
By the time I came across it
the head had already gone.
The rigid description and the older Pantera's
fine body and legs were all that was left.

The rough hand held onto something
I could not make out.
Neither a sword nor a dagger or a cloak pin.
Something curious like a stone or bread.

But all these things I never said to him.
His father we thought was an honourable carpenter,
not occupying militia, though black armour
still lay in the shadow of the workshop.

His mother being so revered, the secret
was not for his enemies' eager ears.
I don't think he really wanted this.
As we sat to eat the space he left
for what everyone thought was God's place
was in fact for a mortal presence,
forty years of service in the 1st cohort of archers.

He would keep a close eye on the legionaries
and made friends there, for our dry and hot land was alien territory
to those used to a temperate climate and good company.
Often he would whisper for small information,
and equally small queries would go about the garrisons.

He consorted with whores and soldiers
for both good and desperate reasons.
Sinners cast an obscure but radiant shadow.
But it was hopeless. The man was far away;
miles off in the northern territories,
riding further and further from
that last hot and tedious tour of duty.

Disciple

No one recognised the name,
though I mentioned it four or five times
in the market square.

No one recognised the name,
and regarded me eventually with suspicion,
so I decided it was time to keep quiet.

I had not seen the body,
and could not believe what was said.
All I had seen was a suffering man

not necessarily death.
And besides I did not want that death.
My life was better occupied

searching for the better alternative.
It could be that he wanted silence now,
and all that I wanted was —

his breathing next to mine,
his hand in my hand,
and the end of this loneliness.

Night-time came and no one would lodge me.
So I carried on walking
until I could see the hillsides in shadow,

hunting a trail I had no idea how to track,
for an animal I had never seen,
in a world where all food is gathered,

not by spear and stealth,
but by simply reaching out a hand
to trees full of fruit.

Stolen

'they gave large money unto the soldiers, Saying, Say ye,
His disciples came by night, and stole him away while
we slept.'

(Matthew XXVIII, v.12-13)

It was a defensive story, I know.
What could I do but end my account
with the great and hopeful wish that brought
sense and patience to our empty hours?

I never witnessed the miraculous claims
and even those said to be at the tomb
could not distinguish their longing
from their hard and pitiful grief.

But when the ink is steady at my hand,
I also whisper for you.
And as surely as those who saw the bread
upon your tongue I feel a warmth
within my palms, but that is all.

How could I have ever known
that one man's touch would open up
my clutching fingers? The children I brought
into this world to comfort and to occupy
were kissed and then forgotten,
because here there was no waiting,
no cautious plan was wanted.
I simply closed those sterile ledgers
and stole myself away.

Reading of miracles and the cities we entered
my family must surely understand
the cruelty of my long confinement.
I leave my defensive story then
for the home I left so rashly,
not thinking of my empty hands
or the bread I stole for hunger.

There is no place of consolation.
No book can silence the change in me.
The voices in the market streets
repeat with all your fruitless words,
and I cry for what was briefly held
then stolen while I slept.

James

He was speaking of the arguments they had
and how it was beyond healing now,
and someone else's message had gone out
to the ports and cities stripped of his own word.
And I found it difficult to console him,
and learned over time that it is wrong to console;
despair is real and necessary for that man.
And even I have lived long enough
to hear his name fade into a list of dissenters
without voice or face and their books burnt.

He asked me for some water and a small leather bag
he kept in a chest in the other room.
I had to pour the water between his yellow lips.
He was too weak even to loosen the cords on the bag.
He wanted to show me something.
I was new to the city then and visiting family
found myself tending this curious stranger.
I had learned under good doctors and was assumed
thereby, to be of some hope. So I tended as best I could,
understanding a little of what he said but not understanding
the old and broken things he lay before me;
bits of cloth, ancient bread, a small document, some hair.
It was like a lover's collection.
He asked me to put them in his hand,
and as I did so his eyes closed.
I sat there waiting, watching him hug these poor things,
before his hand loosened and sleep took him.

I was glad I was not at his death which,
like so many of his friends before him, was brutal and ugly.
I was told not to mention the things he had held,
for surely they would be taken away,
altered and claimed for some other party.
They were best forgotten. And I was not to mention his name
in certain company or that I had ever spoken to him.
He was a fine man but misguided,
who died a martyr and blessed our leaders.
We must maintain this story at all times,
for none of us would wish to die like him,
and all of us would, in this way, be truly remembered.

Simeon

On his death his place was taken by Simeon
who was afraid but would not refuse.
For a short time Simeon kept them together in the city;
but for him, as for everyone else in the capital,
the course of events seemed clear and inevitable.
At last they left, selling nothing,
simply leaving at night with no note.
They are said to have crossed the river and headed north,
basing themselves in an obscure, unfrequented town
that even now is sand and goats amongst rubble.
Some of us have heard stories that they continued to withdraw,
wandering far into valleys and river basins
that must have been promised land to them,
so lush and equitable.

Divorced from us and our petty, violent arguments,
they spoke among themselves a dialect and debate
we had soon cast off and ignored.
They preserved their traditions caring little if we scoffed,
for we were a long way off and each day forgetting more.
Of course, Simeon's prudence in leaving the city was fully justified.
Serious fighting broke out very soon after.
Troops ran amok murdering our friends, our mothers and fathers,
and a siege began that ended, predictably, in bodies and fire.

So I think I was also glad to leave and regretted disagreeing with
    Simeon.
I think I would rather be with him, tilling that lush valley,
my name obscure and my head full of his strange observances
than in this patch of parched earth, righteous, justified,
and sick at heart.

Thomas the Twin

'Thomas spoke among the Parthians. He was said to have died at
Mylapore, near Madras in India, pierced with lances.'

Even as a child I was jealous of my brother.
I held his cloak while he engaged in some argument,
some clean example of his life and will.
I was simply contrast to his charisma, his insight,
the piercing thought which my tongue could not follow.

I sat in the shadow and gathered up our belongings,
arranged lodgings, maintained good relationships
with the local authorities, and ushered the gathering crowds.
I cherished a proud fantasy and would place my cloak
on top of his at each synagogue, or compete
for the women's attention, sadly abusing the similarity of our looks.

When we arrived in Paphlagonia for the wedding of King Andrapa
he wanted me to travel elsewhere, far ahead of him.
'Do not be afraid,' he said, 'my grace is with you.'
And I kept up my refusals for what would I become
far from his person? And what would I say
from the inspirations of my own tongue, not his?
I could imagine only blank faces or laughter,
and the anticipation of disgrace checked me.
I was sold a slave to the merchant Abban,
'parting with a sum of three pounds of unstamped silver'.
This way, he said, I would safely arrive at my destination.
But my contraband status pricked the old wound
and my rage at night would not be stilled.
I did not wish to turn my toe in the dust 'amid alien corn',
expecting as I did, glory and a light to fall surely upon me.
I wanted everything that was coming to him to come to me,
not this exile among barbarians, and God's dark answer
to all my prayers, to those foolish wants,
here at Mylapore, near Madras, in India.

Visitor to Longinus

'In legend Longinus was the captain at Golgotha. He also super-
vised the soldiers on watch at the grave. After the resurrection
Longinus received the shroud and was consecrated as a Bishop
in Cappadocia.'

I was a conscript and found the coarseness
of my barrack-room companions more than I could bear.
All of it seemed spitting between obscenities,
and I could not understand it.
Surely I (a sensitive child much given to scripture
and pious looks at service) was singled-out
for the priesthood, not for these banal duties
amid lawless foreigners; a butcher's boy
bagging the latest revolt's shattered heads.

Still, I received one duty I could stand,
an early morning sentry at the crucifixions.
This is where they said I received my call,
though, in reality, it was the centurion
and not me (a lowly soldier) who passed
the dying man that valuable potion,
grazed his side with the lance
and spoke the famous words.
He went on to become Bishop of Cappadocia.
I simply fell asleep at the tomb and woke up,
some years later, to a secular life and an undeserved fame.

I visited Longinus in Cappadocia to ask him of those times
and his new life. My memory was coloured
by resentment and I recalled nothing
but routine and therefore dull events.
He was a gentle man despite the years of military service
and what had turned
out to be a persecuted life
(his arms I could see were a mass of scars).
He showed me a long, linen cloth
and a collection of his religious writings.

His church seemed poor and unorganised to me.
The temple was a hut amid arid rock.
Nevertheless, I was not the priest I wanted to be,
and sought advice from any religious officer.

He said that he could tell me nothing,
though perhaps I had never seen a religious community.
So he showed me round his foreign parish,
his ragged congregation and his cell;
a bare room, a bed, some water and fruit,
and high in the corner Caesar's honour
to the centurion Longinus for successfully crushing
yet another Jewish revolt.

Clement to Theodore

for Morton Smith

'When Mark wrote the first gospel it is possible that he deliberately witheld certain teachings. After Peter's death in Rome Mark went to Alexandria, staying with Clement, where he wrote his book again.'

I remember his careful hand at night.
He added stories to those already written,
and sayings which he knew would lead us all
to that innermost sanctuary.

He left his composition to our church
and died at last, his labour done,
and I could breathe once more having seen the peace
that came to rest upon his eyes, his hands still at last.

Theodore, I miss him greatly,
and his book, which it is my duty to guard,
feels like a lock of the beloved's hair.
I carry it to my pillow at night.

Not all true things are to be said to all men.
His words would wither in a cynic's mouth,
and I could not bear that. It is harsh
but let the fool walk in darkness.

Where the spirit of the Lord is, there is liberty.
I have seen the earth turn to dull ash,
and the bones of my skull become my prison wall.
That shall not happen again.

Now I know the meaning of the story kept by him,
of Our Lord taken to a garden in Bethany,
full of an anger that rolled the great stone.
I think of the youth stretching out his hand,

and his hand being seized.
'The youth looking upon him, loved him,
and began to beseech him that he might be with him.'
I would be with him at that moment,

woken from the dark interior
to the hand of a man whose rage had rolled
away the stone. And I think of him
as with opened eyes seeing anew
that garden, that shining human face.

Unwritten Episodes

This part is not written about.
After the death that did not occur,
and the great funeral that never happened,
he entered a long valley on foot
and, like the rest of us, became a journeyman,
picking up bread and money here and there
whilst the enthusiasts began their elevations,
first as a voice, then as a book.

Meanwhile, like us all, he is ageing,
making and breaking friends, loving, hazy,
unspecific in recollection, having a small house
and debts before moving on,
finding a stumble in his heart, consulting,
falling silent at night and remembering
what now seems a long time ago and a different man.

The book is already written,
and its passage through various eager hands
in cities with many traders,
ensures his name will live forever
apart from his person;

which is now stiffening in a poor shelter
somewhere far off and his memory indistinct
and his friends few and uncertain,
some illiterate, some grateful for an ear.

And later, followers pass through
a small town and a graveyard.
His body is under a stone and the name
is one they do not recognise.
They pass on their journey to another place,
redolent of someone else's birth and someone else's death,
neither belonging to this stage post, to this place
where we pay for our meal, stow our rubbish and move on.

An Old Costume and an Old Book

> 'he slipped out —
> just like an actor who,
> the play over,
> changes his costume and goes away.'
> (C.P. Cavafy, 'King Dimitrios')

So I have come to a quiet place and a still room
for the silence after so many words spoken,
forgotten now, as I am an old man and my name
revered elsewhere, the person assumed dead.

I stand up in a far country holy and made of gold.
I am present as a strong wine, bought as a book
and placed upon the most precious shelf of the house.

Here, I am a tax-payer's burden.
I make expeditions for food
and return at night neither to write nor to read,
but to watch the fire and sit.

Elsewhere I have ascended into heaven
which is simply an empty room and a fire,
for what God provides none of us want,
and should we see it, we turn our faces away
and set about the task of creating
what we should have, what we really deserve,
not this paucity and silence.

Never mind. I am far off now
and my age is no reminder of my youth.
The journeys I made, which were extended exits,
are over now. The Lord, my God, sits
in a parcel of straw ready for collection.

I am waiting to be gathered up and returned
to what I was before speech left my mouth.
The important word cannot be spoken.
It is not a word at all,
and that saddens me, an old man, far away
from my extraordinary successes, my world-turning successes,
my triumphs, my sufferings, my great and meaningful death,
cast off like a suit of actor's clothes.

Given Word

I

Each day the villagers
leave a covered bowl at my door.
They do not treat me like a holy man,
and I confess I am not,
but holy ones put me here.
So in respect for them,
or because of my appropriate dress,
they leave food for me.
It is simple usually;
a little fish, some fruit,
raw vegetables, a rough
thumbed-out bowl half-full of wine.
I live on that for most of the day
and tend my half-hearted crops
in the shade outside.
I have never done anything
like this before
having an over-resourceful mother
and still young.

There are fish to catch.
I have hooks and line,
though I am afraid to go out
now the shipments of parchment
and ink have come in
and I must work my learning
to some profit.
At this time of year
the evenings are long,
as I was told, the weather mild.
I like to sit on a battered chair
in front of the door
and watch the finches play
and the sun come down

and forget about the bundles
and ink inside.
I like to remember,
and I like not to remember.
I am disappointed.
I have led a disappointing life.
But now I have been given something
to kill that disappointment;
or so I feel.

Lemons and orange leaves,
figs and olives,
the food, the paper and the ink
all rest together.

II

It is so quiet I could hear steam slip from the waters.
I collect the bowls together,
write simple, spaced lines.
I feel the heaviness of my wrists
yet bring everything to my mouth
because, sadly, I am still a child –
my pen, my fingers.
I see the stars fall very softly.
They burst with little spurts of flame.
As they hit the earth each leaves
a tough little cinder which is the dead star.
I always thought the God I knew was gentle and wise,
that he was a kind father and a loving mother.
I felt confirmed in this. But He said,
'what I say is always the truth,
it is always the death of something.
When you dream I reply not according
to your wants, but mine.'

And I know heaven is only for the brave.
No hearthfire, no patchwork or birdsong.
There is nothing we could wish for,
nothing we could want.

III

I live in one room lit by a wood fire
and turn a stew in the copper.
I collect shellfish at low tide,
keep a sparse diary and construct the book
I was sent to make. Papyrus and ink bowls,
the stylus still dry, the dirt,
powder and water, still untouched.
A fisher but inexpert in sail,
I made enough to eat.
With no wife or daughter I followed
because these pearly fish blistering in the sun
could not sustain me. I tasted an unknown
flavour and would eat.
I could not name it, nevertheless
I am here to pronounce it.

Each morning I wake up early and set about
the chores, eat some bread, drink a little,
count the arc of the sun. The villagers
are sleeping behind their olive shutters
whilst I return to the high easel, as I remember,
and write nothing.

Words are given life on the tongue.
The tongue eats, it kisses.
I rake the embers, chew some crust,
fall on the straw bed.
Cotton rags frame the window.
There will be starlight tonight,

the hush of the sea and no words at all,
no swift sail.
I was left with a promise
and love's recollection;
it has not been enough.

There is food to collect today
and walls to repair.
We get what we deserve.
There is sacrifice to be had for money earned.
Words collecting outside like litter.

III Pagans

Hades

I watch the auguries stumble into the underworld.
They have dark and fathomless eyes;
cattle, calves, a white hart,
I cannot understand them.
I lift a frail hoof, repair the dry torn flesh
about their stomachs as best I can.
But I cannot answer their eyes,
or explain the bewilderment that has come to them.

The small spring at my hand tumbles carelessly.
A blessing to men they say.
Like the evening nurse preparing a draught
that I pass into your hand, saying I wanted you
and your breath close to me like a clear word;
but, in truth, I cannot hurt you.

Enter the fields now, and forget.

The Wedding Cup

The chapel gardens open at twilight
and secretive herbs growing close to the ground
offer no flurry of blooms, only the awkward cascade
of their stems and ragged leaves
before that expansive and eloquent smell.

Like the story there are two springs in the garden.
A soul who drinks from the sweetest fountain
will enter fields of grey blossom and forget.

The church is small and white
with a path trodden up to the door.
The altar is a low table where the faces turn in.
As I wait alone I notice little tin plates
displaying a leg or an ear.
They are the deposits of a prayer
for the sister's wound, the father's operation,
the hurt in the family.

And in Bath one day I saw the same pains
scrawled in Latin on pewter plates:
'Sulis Minerva save my mother, heal my father,
curse the bastard who stole my purse.'

Is it forgetfulness I want
when there is another spring here?
Someone takes my hesitant hand.
All she can offer is water,
clear and bitter like remembered hurts.

In the garden the leaves turn their pale undersides to the wind.
They twist like a flurry of vapours,
like a dream of enfoldment before darkness.

Asphodel

I am sitting in an open field,
drinking water by a still pond.

Mist has settled on my hands.
My hands are full of grey water.

The pond reflects the low sky
and I am quiet now, the running over.

My hands fall to my sides.
The grey blossoms

fleece the fields
and pacify with their ghost faces.

A sudden wind stills
like the shades who lie down

to sip quietly at the pond sides,
to sip blood like men at last

given unpoisoned water,
drinking forgetfulness in the meadows

of tall sprouting asphodel.
The colourless blossoms like veils,

grey, pearl-like, intermittent.

Greek Tombstone

Two men greet each other.
They clasp each others' hands before turning.
It is a farewell to the dead
among asphodels and pomegranates,
cypress trees and still water.

No one hunts here.
The deer do not run, fleet and delicate.
There is no noise,
only the presence of thunder,
the brother of thunder,
that space between sound and an arrow of light.

Don't forget to take with you
two pieces of barley bread soaked in honey
and two coins in your mouth.
Turn your face from the man
whose load has fallen from his ass.
Turn your face from the man
who raises his hand in distress
from the cold river.
Turn your face from the women weaving cloth.
Help none of them.

This is my advice:
pay for your crossing,
take the coins I pass into your hand;
pacify the beasts that would maul you
with sops of honey.
Soon you will come to a simple building
where a woman waits to greet you.
She will offer you a great banquet,
but that is not for you.
We are not of her table.
Take a small crust of bread and eat.
What comes to us is the ground
and common bread, nothing more.
She gives only to the fortunate,
something they may hold but never open.

Message (Calypso)

I come to a courtyard beneath high cypresses,
and there is a mosaic of broken shells
surrounding a spring where my companion waits.
He is dabbling a hand in the clear water,
curious of his cool fingertips, wiping them on his knees
as he sees me and begins to get up.

He offers me a board with a message scratched in wax.
We are silent for a moment as I wipe my eyes,
hoping for clarity and the words to be otherwise,
but they are obstinate and unforgiving.

My friend draws little spirals in the water
and does not raise his eyes to mine.
Eventually he paces out of the courtyard,
leaving me to the circle of this familiar regret.

There is nothing I can do.
I have forgotten to expect your warm hand
in my palm again. Stepping through empty rooms,
I know you wait for guests to arrive.
But by morning it is strangers who console you;
taking your tight hands, nodding to your complaint,
leading you out to the clear fresh air.

Every one of your prayers may reach me.
And each one may stir sand under the sea
of my travelling. But I cannot come back.
The waters are calm here and the sun is kind.

My companion calls me out of the courtyard
to a table beneath the trees' shade.
He has laid out four fishes and a glass of water.
I eat with his hand on my shoulder,
thankful for his considerate distractions.

Tomorrow we shall go to the coast and swim.
No complaint can reach me there.
We are simply two strangers laughing in the shallows,
then striking out for the open bay,
where the turning currents dissolve my cares,
like the features of your forgotten face.

Company

You had studied in your youth and then run wild.
The chaotic spirit led to this dark house.
Reduced to four walls and a locked door –
surely no one could possibly reach you.
You wanted to hide, I understood, from a cut
in your life that could not be explained.
This house is your refuge from that inexplicable meeting;
the accident which, we could all escape.
(Though all the time you ensured with each closed shutter
the intimate presence of that familiar companion.)

I walk from the orange groves to the open arches.
I want to hear good counsel because
when this man speaks people gather round
as we would all gather round a fire at night
when it is cold and there is no shelter.
Invisibly he walks with those of us
who keep to the courtyard with our books.
I think of him not at the fall of snow
or the remorseless dark engine, but when
I put my hand into water, or when, with a friend,
we are joined by her companion, strange to me.

The Tyrrenhians

When he sat on the deck,
I was afraid to contradict
the orders of my captain.

'Rope and sell the bastard'
I said nothing.
The helmsman turned from us in disbelief.

I had spent my childhood by water;
the construction of ships, their great beached bows
like the heads of whales breathing tar, bitumen.

My father turned from the sea
to his desk and scales,
said nothing.

My mother worked hard, she did not stop.
When discomforts and pain came to us,
she turned her face and scrubbed.

I drifted out of the colleges of young men
into the town's trade,
merchant ships stitching the islands like bad linen.

We were broached by pirates,
and our oil and cloth taken.
I threw myself in with these disappointed men.

I feared their imagination for torture
on my still tender skin,
but wanted cruel employers, cynical and sure.

He is sitting on the deck saying nothing.
Something is wrong; there is quiet
proceeding from something other than fear.

It is the silence of a man detained by wayfarers.
He is in curious argument
before settling it, knowledgeable and accurate.

They clamour with ropes
that simply fall from his limbs.
I turn from my pail of water

to see a single tender bud pierce the deck floor.

Holy Places

Eleusis ditched by cement factories.
Hopkins mourning a butchered tree.
The Nemian spring, scant rubble,
a dribble and a gelati store.
Windsor Great Park, a private golf course,
the oak fenced off.

The holy places have shifted,
edged off, lit in a cluster
of weeds or fungi gathered
like a village in the moist ditches;
or on the high street, there they are,
impersonal, lovely.

Audience

I sat away from the trade door,
certain that if I squatted here,
face to the brass plate,
she would come from the crowd
that talked so eagerly of her
to talk to me.

I was busy.
I was busy placing dust
from one shelf to another,
sipping at tea,
letting the sun rest on my hand,
refusing to turn my eye to her.

Surely she must see.

Visitor after visitor came,
and I thought myself content
to pass small talk and small silence
with her imitators, her well-wishers,
those who wished for rest
only in those arms.

Each passed from me, finally
to enter the curtained room
and the scent of her
collecting like spice.

One day as I sat in the hills
listening to the women call to each other,
controlling their cattle with an accurate stone,
I saw her pass in the valley opposite,
and in my joy, for the only time,
got up and shouted and waved,
and hearing me she turned, waved back,
beckoned me to come.
Her face seemed one-hundred feet from my own.

I did not reach the valley till dusk
when darkness came like a door, solid and black.

IV Heavens

Rescuer

(for L. Lee)

The sun moves slowly across the open floor
as I take water in my cupped palms
from the broken pipe that drips above me.
Each day, a girl brings a small piece
of unleavened bread. She passes it through the doorway
in silence. Whiter than her little hand,
it is flavoured by the fragrance of her touch;
better than white soup and the coarse loaf
that served for food at home, a room and the silence
broken only by my spoon tapping the basin.
I spent my days forgetting events that split
the skin of my palms. Now at least,
in this bare room, I am alone and free.
The thin blankets ease my head and I
can settle to a long and dreamless sleep.

When that lock was finally broken and I smelt
the perfume of this strange and foreign air,
it was like her singing now in the white courtyard,
her voice rising perfectly, the pure note
of a full life denied me. I would be happy
simply to stay in the lodging that is her eyes
and song, to eat the bread that smells of her
and drink the sure voice that soothes me
like her open and forgiving hand.

Heaven

I was there simply to serve tea and meals at regular hours, to be
silent, to ask no questions, only to bring her tray to the kitchen
where white bread was placed on a china plate, a tiny round-nosed
silver knife, a glass half-full of water and a pile of small sugared
pastries. I was to take this meal to her at 9, again at 2, and finally at
7. She was understandably pale and would sit by the window. The
heavy brown shutters were always closed, but there was a flap she
could open to peek at the world outside as if waiting, a little
anxiously, for the longed-for companion. When I was let in I had to
stand by the door for a few seconds and allow my eyes to adjust both
to the darkness and to the brilliant square of light that illuminated
her dark mouth.

I walked across to her small wooden table and laid out the
refreshments and napkins. She would always say thank-you to me, a
little absently, before sipping the water and returning to her square
of light. I never knew how tall she was because she never stood up,
and the only impression I got of her clothes was their simplicity,
falling in soft lines from her delicate shoulders. I served her in this
way for a number of weeks, growing more and more eager to at least
say something, some question, some word of comfort to her though
I knew it was forbidden. And when finally I did open my mouth she
turned to me with narrowed eyes. Later she greeted the soft red fruit
I placed in the middle of her white plate with pursed lips and hard
swallowing, hiding her face in shadow before beginning to speak:

'Once I prayed to the Virgin to allow me to taste the delights of
heaven. Whilst walking through the municipal gardens I saw a
spring of pure water and heard the song of a small bird, a tiny voice
that delighted me. And, as it continued, so a soft woman's voice
answered the bird, singing high and clear, threading the bird's song
with human warmth. When both voices finally faded and hunger
drew me back to my apartments, everything had changed. In the
space of that duet the cast had fallen from my eyes and suddenly the
world pressed upon me with a weight of sensation I could not bear.
The simple evening light felt like depths of water encasing my face,

the tap of my shoes on the bare floorboards boomed like infernal drums in my ears, and I smelt the rank odours stamped indelibly upon my tainted person. No one could ever sing to me for blood appeared at my broken eyes. The Virgin is poor and innocent because heaven is her respite from the pandemonium we inhabit. Her delights can only be heard in this closed, secluded room where I withdraw to my chair and this waiting.

'As I sleep a voice answers the sad query I repeat in the empty courtyards. It brings me to soft woodlands and a pool as still as the broad night sky. When I look into the water I see another face, besides my own, watching gravely. She asks for the touch of my face on her fingers, for my feet on the soiled bed of her garden. But I fear the grip of that dark hand, waking to the safety of my sure enclosure and guilt of the promise I so nearly embraced.'

As she spoke I could hear the birds singing outside and the plash of water. The denial of her life had closed my ears and I longed for the touch of her mouth upon me. I thought of her long wait for the answering voice to free her, should it ever come to this darkness where the food I bring can only please with its taste of nothing at all.

Relief

'According to some historians, after the revolt in Jerusalem was crushed, the Romans sold the women captives into slavery. Some ended up as prostitutes in the bankside brothels of Londinium.'

You must listen when I tell you
of things stolen from my keeping,
when the high fires stilled my mother's hands
and ashes soft as her careful fingers
fell about my sleeping head.
Cinders still glowed in the temple precinct
when all the women around me
were gathered into arid compounds
and I was taken for a face
I did not choose. My mouth was locked
as my body spoke in that terrible sweat,
and I longed for fragrant water
cool upon my torn fingers
before despatch and the dark ocean
that passed beneath my sleeping
like the memory of relief.

When I was sold I was made to strip.
As they exchanged their coins
some felt my flesh between finger and thumb,
pressing their nails into my open mouth,
masturbating as they turned me about.
I supposed that a thick-set body
without charm meant death.
So I spoke the music of my foreign tongue
into the ears of my purchasers,
explaining my clear advantage,
what cannot be passed over,
what relief may come to them
from this breath upon their fevered ears.

They listened when I told them
of thoughts they dare not voice
which meant this naked body
was passed from my tender keeping
to a bunk, a straw pallet
and this cold, damp quarter.

Now my heart flies out to my mother's hands,
to her skin unpunctured beneath my fingers,
to what was said to me in trust
over late fires when our doors were shut
and a calm so deep came within my sleeping
that I always seek this one location.

> *From a garden of fragrant trees*
> *I came to a room relieved of darkness.*
> *There I felt the marvel of my hands*
> *flexing at my simple wish.*
> *The door had opened and my mother*
> *came in and sat on the bed's corner.*
> *She turned her head to listen*
> *to the warmth of my breathing*
> *which was filling my throat.*
> *And she was speaking to me but*
> *I could hear nothing, and asking*
> *for her speech the words of her*
> *calm sentence fell about my hearing*
> *like water through my fingers.*
> *She brought her mouth to my ear*
> *explaining so slowly and easily*
> *what must come to me, what cannot*
> *be passed over, smiling gently now*
> *as she spoke into my ear because*
> *the words must be poured in*
> *carefully and not a drop spilled.*
> *Then she stood up and she laid*
> *a palm to my forehead, as if testing*
> *for the curious fever and for relief*
> *in my swift and merciful delivery.*

The calm passed from me like the dun river
and its cargo of sullen, moneyed men.
They come for the curiosity of my skin,
and for the scent of their homelands in my dark hair.
I welcome them only for the mothers they call upon
as they whisper their relief, taking my hand
to the fevered heat of their sleeping heads.

Burial

'In Colchester, local women who married men of the occupying Roman army were buried in the Roman style.'

I took a retired man as my patient husband
and he was slow in his years but tender,
the small wounds of his service
stayed as amusements for us both.
But when bed became the home of my sickness
his legions' pay provided for the decorated lead
that is my ship on this solemn journey.

He thought of me with care, placing at my head
my favourite rings and bracelets, a flask of perfume,
and some pins to set my long red hair.
Our friendship was too brief and I spent too many years
fearing the brutality of his foreign arms
before I was taken into them like a child at play.

Now he lives in one empty room
and shapes a childish straw to feed me.
At the time of his regular visit, an egg
or some shellfish pass over my hard lips,
followed by the salt and honey of his familiar breath.

He fortifies me not for my silent companionship
but for a sleep that has taken all my talk.
I know this love is convalescence.
Soon he will leave for other lands and other women.
What I receive is the hard passing
of this world's attention as I face the next,
well-presented and well-fed, expecting no love
or ornament from the foreign arms that surround me.

Not With Us

This heaven is so still. There is an orange grove
laid out formally in rows and a floor of intricate mosaic.
The ghost fruit trees do not need rain anymore,
but I assume because it is serene and beautiful
the delicate irrigation channels have been kept
and water sings gently underneath
the heavy branches. I walk here at night
surprised to find that I have kept my appetite
taking the round oranges that taste
only of the water that feeds them
and the white bread so neatly
laid out on the stone tables.
Now and then there are big, blue olives to sample,
but I often put them to one side.
It is a shame to clutter this place with stones.
The weather is so mild that after circling
the inner courtyard some fifteen to twenty times
I lay my head on the ground and fall asleep.
My dreams are full of talking people.
Someone pats my shoulder, kisses me goodbye,
and I wake to find their flowers folded up in my hands.
Though I am well looked after I long for company,
not crowds or even a rowdy group
drinking and shouting, just a few companions,
amiable and mild, to spend the pleasant hours
underneath the green canopies.
I think the garden must be new
and I a favoured inhabitant here before
the tape has been cut and the busy citizenry
enter talking like shoppers.
When milk is available I like
to make pretend tea for them with the ice-cold water
and little metal jugs for pots and cups –
singing old songs I knew gently to myself
before night and this strange and crowded sleep.

Hospice

A dry tablet and distilled water.
We put on white starched gowns,
like sheets on old furniture,
and pad through the ornamental gardens.

In my room I have a wooden bowl
containing walnuts, a yellow cheese,
crab apples, and also a jug of milk.

I rest under linen sheets
and through the cruciform of my window I see
the swaying of cypresses,
the winds smooth over the ponds and rose beds,
golden carp still in their grey pools.

Ragman

I was in a beer shop in Heneage Street
full of the grubby traffic that frequented this quarter,
heaving their sacks onto the counter
for weight, examination, and the pennies that followed.

Sometimes one would press the bar and take a pint.
He usually sat in silence, staring at the floor
as if he expected to find in quiet examination
some other fallen rag and so make up the livelihood
already draining his slow glass.

I asked him what he thought about as he trudged along,
eyes fixed to the paving stones' brief horizon.
He answered, 'Of nothing.'

'Better than remembering the hard waking
that must come before I go out to the street
and prod among the piles of rubbish
that surround these cold tenements.

'Now and then I pick out something that surprises –
a square of clean linen, a bright orange silk.
I hold this up to my eyes
before taking it across my face
like a soft and tender hand.

'Such nothings fill up my greasy sack.
I drink and settle my thoughts
before the days' labour ends,
turning to my bare lodging
for sleep in the unoccupied hours.

'All I have for bed-linen is a pile of old sacks,
but alone at night, from my bag of nothings,
I bring fire-coals, caresses, the bright salamander,
and heaven's blue fabric as soft as the sea.'

Open Water

You know I am circumspect and cautious by nature,
but I feel healthy, though I am still at port,
and the familiar routines occupy my time.
Spring has arrived and I gather up my belongings,
for soon the sea I long for will arrive.

Each day I spend a little time on the boat,
practice the bunk and watch the lamp rock.
It will be some time before I am free to leave harbour,
but the sting of salt on my tongue is enough.
I wave at the boats now as they plough through the surf
and I cannot envy them.

I turn from my desk to a pitcher of wine.
It is my pleasure each afternoon to drink
and to feel the cradle of the hold beneath me.
I imagine the river estuary broadening,
the harbour walls sinking and the coastline
a grey ribbon that twists to nothing.

I feel her keel tug at my heart
as I turn my head toward the horizon
and the landscape held in my imagining
like a winter seed.

The Quartermaster keeps regular hours,
and my reverie breaks at two,
but even his load seems light,
as each stroke of the pen, each passing bale
brings me closer to that cool evening,
our farewells,
                    and open water.

V   Others

Fear of Open Water

I am terrified of water.
I cannot bear it. I mean the depth.
Even the clouds sit like coupled links of heavy chain.

Our unstable craft sways in the still harbour.
Will you take the rudder for me?
I can tell by the strength of your arm
what fortitude, what forthright line
you would maintain on our slow journey.

I feel in that swell the rocking of a ghastly cradle.

I have heard everything you say,
the glittering bay so fragile a curtain,
it will pass through my fingers.
You change the dread before sleep
into still shelter. I will not let you go.

I carry you into my bunk at night,
after this world of brutal strangers,
of empty activity and the passing hours.

Mutineer

They pushed the boats off the soft sand
into the swell, and my cries of anger
dispersed into the gulls calling,
so I knew that as I woke each morning
I would hear that fury and disgust,
and my new response – a clipped breathing
into the sacking that covers me.

My great day was to turn from my vain sea-gazing
and face in to land.
All I wanted to watch was empty sand
and not the grave trees behind me.
So I am turning now
away from my pebbles and eye-shade,
away from my temporary encampments.
I could not let myself believe
I would be here so long.

Drink

The smooth taste of salt oil mashed with grain
to make a paste that ferments.
After some months in a dark cell, built for the purpose,
the keeper hauls out five fat jars and pours.

I placed my trouble in the dark earth
and now wait for the drink to rise.
I wish to be like the keeper, not forgetting,
but tending and studying the brew,
its mood, its bubblings late in the season,
its fizz a sign that all is ready.

I honour it with small ceremonies
and listen with care, sniff the stopper,
shift it tenderly to this or that corner,
into or out of the sun.

Now with the broad cup cool in my palm,
I sink down into long grasses.
The hoops of the olive trees swing above me
and drink warms the dark of my troubled body.
Underneath my arms, the earth
is golden, supported and strong.

A Transitional Object

Each day I go to the cupboard door
to fetch jam or coffee, or some collection I made
in the early summer, fruits and twigs and string,
and visitors think I gather my nervous hands there
for the breakfast that comes before work and the day.
But as I wake I am thinking not of food or work
but what is kept in the cupboard,
smelling deep and rich but only old cloth.
And as I walk into other rooms
there are books and coins and a small brown stone
picked up amongst ruins under the sun
whose rough touch is a signature that all is well.

The passage between the lobby and the guest's room
is lined with curtains and paintings.
At each station, normally occupied by armour,
there is something soft and small.
The timid heart's trust resting there.
And I am placing my hands on each wall
to ensure they are steady,
and the furnishings welcome to my touch,
because at the end of the corridor I see nothing.
And this is the familiar object in my hand,
bringing the world of my certainties
into a world uncertain.

John

I met John only once;
the boy, smiling and curious
about the shining things

that cluttered my desk,
did not know who I was
or what I wanted, yet

he immediately entrusted me
with secrets no one would have told
their most intimate friend.

He danced his dirty little mimes for me
which I never asked to see,
and mouthed the obscene come-ons

I never asked to hear.
He also scratched himself.
I asked if it hurt there –

the place where he scratched –
he assured me he would not go to the police
for me mentioning such things.

He loved toy guns
and his games were full of slaughter.
When he left my office

the floor was littered
with miniature car-wrecks,
and the corpses of dolls.

What could I prescribe
but a course of treatment
his parents would never assent to paying.

'This is a phase of John's'
I'm sure they would say,
as they drove him off to those familiar locations

we all recognise on our TV screens;
ordinary rooms, the cheap furniture over-turned,
the dishevelled sheets dotted with blood.

Three Londinium Discoveries

I

The bronze had gone beyond green.
It was now irredeemably black,
like blood two days old.
I could still make out individual wires
between hard clots of rusted metal.
It had been carefully plaited into a scourge
hard enough to break a servant's back.

II

The general had been pensioned off
to this outpost of civilisation
and the climate was not good.
He became morose when the object
of his one pleasure died quite suddenly
in the bankside stews,
not in the glory of his private arena,
thus this marble tombstone.

III

Between the finance houses, the recruitment agencies
and the private gymnasiums – a wooden tablet
buried under the spotless tarmac:
'Take good care you turn that slave-girl into cash.'

Companions

I

Singing into my hands,
calves curious and wary
nose the earth before my feet.
I continue singing for the warmth of it
about my throat.
The animals shift down into sleep.
As the night comes the flame I set
burns steady and pure.
There is no wind.
I have a lake-side of companions
and my breathing steadies to their own.
The deeper stadium of trees watches opposite.
They too are curious,
unaccustomed to music and human smell,
the human company and the hush of animals
sleeping by still water.

II

I imagine a small company about a fire,
coming close, three, four.
Hesitant, careful, they settle down
by the smooth flames snout to tail.
And I am far out at sea,
approaching a dim cove, growing warmer,
greater, as my small boat draws in.
I come to the fire as if only to warm my hands.
They do not move, a place in the circle
has been reserved for me, and I take it
as a stray come in to sudden and strange company.
Delicate teeth grip my hand, pulling gently
to a belly of fur, a beating heart.

You and I

An empty glass and a plate of crumbs.
I know we should have dried those late fruits,
kept them for the slow winter months,
a fig or a date to spice our bitter evenings,
anything to keep out this cold.

We walked a long way,
you and I, on the cold sand-line.
We picked through the stones and driftwood,
the dry carcasses and salt fleeces
still not daring to touch.

The wind rubbed about the shelter chimneys.
The sea was a low conversation,
caught in the ether, distributed to our ears.
There was speech I could not hear,
a blade of marram that whispered by your ear,

and the stars that marked out their territories
like a slow and great compass.
I thought of all this time you had waited,
impatient, not content, taking small steps,
turning for me when my hand was closer than one simple word.

All this time I have been a pale boy,
clothed in cream linens, fed on pears and almonds,
plucking tiny narcissi from the firm clay
as good as asleep. I did not wish to see you,
still, insistent, a shadow in my nursery.

I only wanted the comfort of my pillow
and a mother's hands guiding me at night,
waking me at morning.
You are dark as the river stones,
delicate and fleet like forest arbours,

like a storm abating, come into the wooden harbour.
How I want to talk now. I want to feel the boats rock
as your body comes in, full, present, and awake.